The Art of Channelling

TANYA TURTON

Copyright © 2024 Tanya Turton

Copyright remains the property of the author
and apart from any fair dealing for the purposes
of private study, research, criticism or review, as
permitted under the Copyright Act, no part may be
reproduced by any process without written permission.
All inquiries should be made to the author.

Typeset & Cover by Chain of Hearts Creative

National Library of Australia - ISBN-978-0-6452064-6-3

The Art of Channelling.

IS this sensation, a divine point of connect that is a promised spirited space that is held within all to speak. A voice of great vibration and uplevelling we shall say upon its reconnect, a description to describe to self to see.

An opportunity of importance unfolds, revealing this as an honouring, a portal, a desire begins to encourage oneself to sit in a restful and relaxed way, to hear, to receive this devoted voice steeped in wisdom as yours in a knowing to remember.

It is in this dear; that you are this courageous human being who is devoted to this journey to remember; the *Art of Channelling*.

The Art of Channelling.

IS the prospect of Channelling. The prospect of Receiving.

The prospect of a deliverance of a Divine Gift is always an implication is it not?

Into ones sensing of righteousness, ones ability, even ones perception of self, for in truth it is a knowing or a known fact that lays heavily present within all if not most of you to feel this ability to rise, to understand of it as an innate voice or conversation to be had or held. To feel many levels of awareness, openings that are to become known to you in this we would describe them to you as an unlocking, a process to feel as one is to dedicate this voice of evolvement to become yours.

For it is a feeling of truth that is to arise in many of you in as a way to describe of self-satisfaction, self-discipline and awareness, an accreditation within oneself to become present in this very moment, this very essence that you would, as we would describe this as your now.

An implication is to lay within many of you, a voice that is to lack this reasoning as to be a well-known proposition within you this self to explain as an interpretation that is to be delivered, offered, or given firstly to oneself in as to describe of self as proper, prosperous, and full. A giveance almost to see of self in this wholesome way, an attitude of self-thought that is to be implemented in as a forgoing of all old attachments, beliefs and interpretations that have held you, bound you, become you. It is yes a way to allow of self to describe of self in as a wanted way, a way to perceive or observe oneself in a new discipline. For it is discipline that must become a prevalence within you to be self-governing within this embodiment of self to describe of self without attachments or without a need to be.

We offer this level of certainty for it to become yours once more.

The Art of Channelling.

IS a god given gift.

A place of higher purpose and power that is to reside what appears outside many of you, unattainable yet ever present for those that are to be asking of it to be seen once more. A tuning into, an alignment to feel of self-becoming balanced again. To describe of it as negative or zero like measurement on a scale that is to stand in perfection neither swaying to or fro and if one does, to have the ability to feel self-pull back in alignment again. It is in here this channelling process that we are to describe of it as such to become yours once more a voice of entitlement, a voice of great description, a voice of great allowance to become, a certainty to sit in this construct, this construct of human embodiment YES; but with a knowing to be more.

A voice of reason is offered here to explain this very being that you are, for in truth and it is in great truth that is yet to be uncovered and unearthed within this self that one must become attuned to this frequency, a feeling, a knowing to describe as passionately yours.

We describe a frequency that is knowing of elaboration. A vision that is to form within oneself to be described as whole perfection, a perfection that is to become yours of truth and understanding. One that is yes to feel as to falter at times, in as a human collaboration to become, but must be allowed to feel as it is to be peeled away in as to suggest the removal of the outer layers, the outer formation that has held many of you in a hardened state of negativity and fear.

The Art of Channelling.

IS simply placed within oneself as voice of contentment, a voice of diverse integration, a placement within oneself once more that is to be initialised and remembered. For it is this voice of opportunity that we are to feel as an impress within this one to use as a description to describe of self in this becoming as a human entity to begin again. We sense this as a commotion within many of you to describe of self as legitimate or to obtain this as a knowledgeable pocket of information. It is in many that we are to describe this as a course or a flush of determination that is to become, that is to overcome those of you that are willing to receive. It is a conversation that is to be held within oneself once more, a placement to describe of this as a willingness, a feeling of contentment and connection to begin again, it is yes held with much hesitation for it is of a nervousness we shall say that is attached to this way to apply that one may receive information in as a {do good way for oneself}.

If one is to feel discord or disharmony within an interpretation of self it will overflow and filter into this ones being causing such feelings of mistrust, and disagreeance. It is to become an allowance of high comprehension we shall say, to feel a flow of interpretation as it is to begin.

When one becomes this truth to believe in again as self to be no longer impressed, inspired or driven shall we say to be of another, it is then in this power that is revisited by you as the remembering of all that you are.

In a sensing of self to be this qualified version to speak in all it is that one is to know, this then becomes likened to a confidence that is to grow and will be revisited often in self- expression to speak.

It is not to be likened to an outlandish ego or voice of descript to boom, but rather a voice deeply entrenched in love, compassion and self knowledge to explore into once more.

The Art of Channelling is this elaborate voice of self-expression in its finest descript of self to speak.

The Art of Channelling.

IS the voice that is to rise.

We offer this word voice as in a human contraption to embody this as a spokes object or spokesperson, to feel a flow of certainty when one is to find oneself sitting to receive a notion or a nudge, a thought of opportunity to speak of self in a grand and knowing way. This is delved deeply into here; this reveal that must beknown as yours, for it is a placement YES that all are of entitlement to enter into again, to be of, to stand within and it is this impress that many of you are to feel a certainty of once that connection has been made or allowed to be revived or relived. When one can use words such as love, purpose, promise, divine divinity in a description for self to trust, it becomes an opening, an awareness and an emerging into again as a proposition to become yours. For one must be certain of a particular range of frequency or deliverance within self to comprehend or connect to again. It is a voice of promise yes; of promise in this that you are this attainability once more, to believe that you are this purposeful being, this energy of great magnificence. This truth spoken, this openness, this awareness that is to become and belong of you again. It is a focal point that we are to delve into here to feel as this is to become entering into once more a space of viability to stand not as in to be corrected, but to be reminded of this that you are elaborate within an essence, a fluid flowing movement or momentum that is to carry you this way.

A resource that has simply been forgotten, that is to be reminded of its magnificent overlay that is yours.

For the *Art of channelling* some would say is an intuition, an innate connection to god source, or a reality of certainty yes it is also a proposition within oneself to perceive again to be this deliverance of voice, to capture self again in this splendor, to speak of self as an alliance within oneself again. To be this deliberate choice, this choosing to see, to uncover, to remember of all it is that one is. We remove the outer layer of existence here, for it is simply a fool hardy way in which it is that one has captured themselves to think of self in this as a human prospect yes a place of devotion to become and attachment of sorts to progress, an evolvement, an instructed version for you to experience removal we shall say. For it is the removal of all that is good and whole and perfect within you that this endowment has allowed of you to speak of in an uncherished way.

We speak of a higher self here, a higher self that can and is formattable with this energy of belonging, to be a truth speaker, a concept of divine giveance to become yours as in a greater alignment again.

The Art of Channelling.

IS seen as a modality upon this planet earth in this reality, yes a modality of sorts to describe of it as a learned opportunity. A thing of prosperous advancement, a governing within oneself to determine this one qualified enough to receive this as a proposition to begin. But it is a place of humble service and act of disappearance almost within to allow of self to re-evaluate all receiving, all entitlements all becoming's to see through this apparatus that is to hold you present here with a mindful thought concept that you are not or that you need.

It is a progression through this time space reality to cherish, to encompass, to embrace and unlock this certainty within you again. To use of it as a description to describe of you in this grateful way, for it is in truth, faith, hope and belief that a sensation within you will rise again to feel and to receive this as a certainty to begin. An apparatus that is to never forget.

A Channelling Practise:

Sit now here in a purposeful way, a place or space in allowance to feel to begin. For it is to feel this embodiment as a sensation to begin as an incarnation of a physical being, of a physical realisation, a place, or a home. Bring into your awareness all that you feel present into and of, an awareness and presence that must begin with you. A truth to be told, an unravelling of sorts for it is not to inconvenience us if one is to unravel a little more.

More truths will be told and discovered, they must become the offering as to no longer be held as appendages within self to discover or disclose, they are to become on full display we shall say. To display within this self a truth, a marker of sorts of where to begin. For if one can explore this opportunity, this sensing within self to allow for a new description to become, a new version to speak of self as, we often refer to this as laying all cards out upon the table so all may be upturned and seen.

For it is a space of truth which is to be revealed whether it be a liking or not is up to you. When, and if able to become a space of evaluation with a clear consciousness attached, an opening to see oneself in all propositions that are presented, it is here that it will begin. And a choice or a choosing will be made by you to implement this grand discovery we would call you, your true self, your higher self, your version of love. We are a prosperous ability within you to feel this as a flow of integration, for it is a flow of great compatibility yes that is to rise and become an entwinement or a stirring within you.

It must be allowed to sit easily or steadily in and of you without cause of concern, for it is often this great concern that is attached to the... *Art of channelling*, this gifted voice that is to become your prosperous ever seeing, ever knowing knowledge once more. When one speaks of this in this way it is to become an attunement within oneself, an alignment again.

A dedicated practise of Love. To see of self as to never step out of it, to feel of self fully recognisable of when one is to lean a certain way, is the desirable way. This learning will become known to you once more.

The Art of Channelling.

IS a gift. It is a powerful resource, which is yes an attunement within us the greater essence, the greater being, the greater good that is a natural insight that lays in all that is.

Simply in this as a choosing to be, a knowing, a truth, a power of love.

We give this Art of channelling to be seen as a gift or an opportunity to recognise this within oneself. To provide this as an opportunity to open, to become aware, to awaken, to free this dormant self. For it is in this dormant state that many of you are to reside into, purely as a choosing to remain hidden, to remain resourceful to the human side, the emotional attached addiction that is a fear filled proposition to stand into. For it is this place that many are to reside into purely to receive a concept of self that is yet to be dissolved or discovered. We see the many of you here in this as to be a truth seeker, and it is to imply this way of interaction to the many of you that are to yet feel this dormancy evade the physical form. To become a truth, an encounter we shall say once more, to align self in again.

Self-exploration must become the key to unlock this channelling ability often considered as an intuitive conversation.

We are often considered outside of this version of this human. It is a truth that has been implied and interjected into many of you to feel this as a formidable quest to travel upon or to search within oneself and others to find.

Know that it is not. It is a belonging, an embodiment that is a badge of honour that all shall wear upon its discovery again and upon tuning into this frequency or vibration to realise of self as this powerful receiver, this powerful knower.

For you must all become lessening in this hesitant state to sit to receive. We would imply here a question such as *'What would you fear to see?'*

A truth beknown to you, a voice that has held one down, a hiddenness that is yet to be unearthed or uncovered, a place of descript that one is to despise or distrust, for all embarkments are yours to discover.

And it is in this way that we are to describe you. Simply as this embarkment from the greater being that you are known as to enter here to realise or review of self again in as an opportunity to expand.

Stand steady, presently placed to feel this self in this opportunity to see.

To receive; listen to hear that tiny murmur that divine drop of focused intention to become yours again. Almost like a whisper it will begin.

An opening, an opportunity is described in this to begin as the...

Art of channelling.

The Art of Channelling

IS you.

YOU are the spokesperson of self; are you not?

We ask you in this way; for it is to become a strong direction within you, a defiance almost, held in denial that you are not. One must grab hold of this opportunity again to feel a conquering of a voice that has been misled.

That has been given to self by another, by an opportunity that may have risen in past recollections of self to explore. See self here now as this magnificent opportunity to describe self as an explorer of great contention. For when one is to explore openly and appeal to the governing system that has lived and dwelled within you in as to describe of self as unworthy or unable to see and hear this as your place of truth. We speak this word of truth in as a comparison to many others that are to speak this way. For it is purely an opportunity to suggest to oneself that it is wrong, different perhaps or even misleading. Describe of oneself here, for one must describe of self here as knowing, presently placed, purposeful, and designated to this very essence, for all essences are at times yes an entrapment within oneself to discover and explore but must become a certainty within oneself to be an allowance to become this elaborate performance or perfection to dwell into to remind self of this self-adjustment that is needed.

It is a way we shall say to explain it as likened to a book or a learning of great knowledge that is to lay unfolded yet within you. To feel one certain, to entertain the idea of this becoming, for it must become a turning of the page or an opening of a book of immense interaction that is to begin, to feel to perform again. We implement this idea here to suggest that all shall know upon its point or spot of direct push again, for once one feels this entitlement revealed, this revelation subside within self to explore as an opportunity of disagreeance perhaps, to feel as you are to become this powerhouse, this empowerment to listen, to release all judgment and criticism. Upon knowing of this as a voice of trepidation to begin, you will be aware of this being, this energy of truth, this proclamation that is to reside here in this opportunity.

The Art of Channelling.

IS you, who is to perform not only outwardly, but decidedly within.

Defiantly within in as a vibration that will override and overrule all that has been remembered in a truth that has been not. It is this performance that must become a reconnect again, a plugging into of sorts that you will feel as to have felt a prolonged absence from. A truth or a voice, space, or a place that one stands into in awe. To experience again to feel the dropping away, the nakedness almost, to feel robbed or stripped bare of beliefs that you have carried, as a certainty to have believed yours. When given, yes many of you have attached to these conversations, ideals, or propositions to be, for of what would I be if I were not that. See self-clear now within this opportunity to choose or to be a choice to receive, yes all that is to be presented, all that is to open, all that is to appear written on the pages of this extravagant book of life that you have captured. Read it over and over, revel in it, delve in it, experience it, relive it, see it, for one must become comfortable, one must become unsympathetic to it, unemotional to it, and given in your time yes; you will find a purposeful place to know this no longer can or will capture your attention but to remain there if required by you to revisit but with a lessened attachment. For it is not to forget. It is not to remove, it is not to ask of you to ignore or dissolve this part of you, but yes we are in total agreeance if the situation was to become a becoming once again. But it will be a reveal of intention we shall say that will rise within you when one feels a negotiation to begin to leave or to lessen this receiving or this attachment to the negative or the needless variant that is you.

The purposeful you who has received in this place to now that you have arrived at, the purpose of receiving was to evolve and to expand, to stand present here in observation of self to see. A purpose that is to rise within you, to explore this now, reminding of all that you are, is this grand dedication again. If you have gotten this far and are still delving into the choices, the attachments and the old again; feel self a place to sit, a place to reveal, for it must become this opportunity of exploration that is to become known to you. To allow that which has been given to open, to feel it, to speak of it to acknowledge it, maybe even to embrace.

We speak this way to you; in as a softened state of self-exploration, for it is only you that can do this, it is only you in this purposeful way, as the observer, the seer, the instructor, the director within you that must be called forth to be allowed to be realised.

Are you willing?

The purpose is you, it is a purposeful residing that dwells within all, to see this as a grand advancement in acceptance, for when one accepts of self-one becomes this divine voice of giveance and guidance, a purposeful way to explore this opportunity to self as you are truth in all this as an encompassment within you. You are to become this knowing again it is a placement within many of you that have been given this opportunity to explore to recondition, to dedicate this version this perception of character as an opportunity to explore.

The Art of Channelling.

IS to feel misunderstood at times.

Let us explain.

A feeling of unsettlement arises easily when one is to explore or open all opportunities that one is given to look into and for many will remain hidden until a time of choosing by you to see into. A basic voice or concept of self that will become an elimination to become a grander proposal to feel no longer foolish by what one has held attached to this self to see, hear, be, and do.

But to feel a righteousness appear to feel this mastery emerge out of this foolishness that one has held within self, to describe of self as an in- ability to explore. It is in a hidden timely aspect of you yes; that will be unlocked in direct accordance with this voice that is to allow self to discover to feel captured by again to explore into. A description of self that may not have appeared as right, to feel a dissolving of old attributes, to sense this oppression that has been held onto, and an out of skin like covering to feel raw within this neglect to experience that you have attached to this human voice to be. For one must discover this voice again.

This voice shall be offered as the gift that entices the *Art of channelling*.

Prosperity, Truth & Recognition, are to become the dictations in your day-to-day procedures, to watch as it arrives to a point where it is instantly flipped if you are to get too far from the line of alignment, the lighted version that is deeply defined within you. You are to be sensing this place of power, to feel as it is to overcome you, to impress you with such a certainty that you will be ever reminded of all that you are in yes a simplicity to have begun again, a narrated version of you to explore. If you are still indescribable in this self to explore the *Art of channelling* that is you a voice of rapture & capture to be describable as a love versioned, love visioned impression, then find this space, this place and explore you. Feel what is to rise, this entrapment or contagious energy that is to hold you tight. Explore, revisit, describe, emphasise, and impress this within you. It must be attached to again to see. You must feel this, you must encourage this to rise. It is okay. It is a place of forgiveness that one will arrive at or to, to watch as it is to become a description offered here as a hand-held fan. One that is to open and allow for it to fan outwardly to display, as you are the holder of the handle to see as it is fanned out in front of you taking up the space for you to see it there, describe this you.

Become aware of this you. You are this you in this present moment of descript to be. Settle into this place for awhile for it needs to be seen and recognised.

It needs to be acknowledged as yours. It is okay. It will become an item, subject or topic to be put down in your giveance and your deciding within this self to discover. One must become this opportunity of truth to receive, for it is not of another to discover this for you but it is yours to hold, to manage, to perceive and to carry. It is a blessing of yours to experience, feel to falter or fail, yes it is an opportunity to discover this attachment, this entity that has become yours to describe of self as.

A description that is reminiscent of all that you were.

See self-there now.

For it must be a clearing that is to be done not to say that it will be forgotten, even forgiven, but an opportunity for you to see self in this clear fantastical way, a removal of sorts if one chooses. It is this word foolishness that we attach this conversation to that for it is often upon ones deep reveal of discovering that many of you in human entrapment are to feel this foolishness rise. A foolishness that opens to reveal that one has held this for so long, to be the receiver of great discreditation and disdain within oneself to explore. It is a truth yes that has multiplied and manipulated you, but in only as self to discover and explore. You must become this openness, this awareness, this place of plenty to interrupt self of, for there is no good, bad, divine, or undiscovered it is purely an awakening and opening revealed to step in to explore. It is a hard-pressed place that many of you are to feel as a battle or a combat to have begun, a war that has raged within you for what feels like eons, a truth held hard spot to reveal.

Ask of self why?

Embarrassment is an attachment, a belittling, discomfort, negativity, and where words of scarcity of love are formed. Be here. Real. Be this regulation within self to explore. You must become this choice to discover, for this is the reason the *Art of channelling* is given.

A description within you to feel warranted to become what we speak to offer, to become this knowledge, this truth, this empowerment, this placement within self to be this absolute version of love. It is a simplicity yes; comprehensible at a particular time of your unravelling, a truth that is to be out performing all others and is to appear to discover a sensation within self to reveal this truth, a purpose, a light hearted approach.

YOU are truth, you are a concept of self to explore, you are this beckoning, this calling to again to feel to see and to know and to remember a re-enactment of all others in a divine blessing or gathering.

Use this as a suggestion to begin to feel as one is to sit into this encompassment, this circle or gathering that is to surrender within you an opportunity to explore this *Art of channelling*, this art of purposeful conversation to feel these levels as they are to reveal to you, where it is that you are to sit, where it is you are to embrace self upon, where it is that you are to navigate in and out of with a purposeful voice of gratitude and dedication that is to become yours once more. We are a truth that is spoken, a description to describe this one as a being of love, a voice of recognition that has, is and will be of and always this to describe self as. It is a way of enticement yes; a consideration that must become a place to sit into, to dwell into, to know self again an enlightenment, a lighted version of you.

We are an enrapturing within this essence, to describe this space to you.

The Art of Channelling.

IS yours.

Steady, purposeful, descriptive, indescribable if one is open and ready to receive the truth.

The Art of Channelling.

IS an Art. And If one were to establish this forgotten ancient art, this knowledge, this establishment that lives within you all, in as a sensing of to believe it to be true, you then will remember this gift. It is to be always considered more like an encouragement that is to be yours to offer.

Your god given voice or speech.

It is this that is to be applied to many in as an attachment that is held within, in as a given attitude of possibility, for it is this dire sensing from within that is to lead many of you to appear empty, or to be an apparatus that has not this as a facility within.

It is a becoming yes to feel in a more plentiful way, among many of you upon your planet in this reality that are to assume of self as to be filled with this as a token or a giveance to relive and revitalise within oneself. It is this designation yes in which it is that many of you have come here to perform in this way as an act or service. A discipline to become, a forerunner, a front rower to speak of this as in us to be. It is a sensing from within yes that is to be an establishment that is to grow in an awareness to be spoken of in this as a likened state to be yours.

It is a proposition yes, a voice of prosperity, an enablement to re-enact a quality that is a given right, a sensing from within that is to outperform this in an offering to you by another. It is a voice of coherence, a voice of deliberation, a voice of deliberate essence, in this it is that we are to correct this word in as a hesitation to have become. It is a sensing from within you, to apply this decision, this new way to think, speak and be, that is to become prominent within you in all that are.

The Art of Channelling.

IS a voice to ASK.

It is this sensing from deep within that many of you are to hold this spot to feel a place likened to a pit that is to sit deep within. Allow of self here now to acknowledge this as an opportunity to begin. To allow of self to view inward if necessary, allow of self to view this space this place, this deep void, this vat, with the ability to assume, imagine, and decide that it is a vision that you hold within. This place or concept of thought to become yours to feel revisiting again, to revitalise this energy, this essence of love.

For it is a space of awareness that is. It is this space of awareness that holds this *Art of channelling*. This voice of descript that describes of you to be magnificent, an observation in plenty and in all, to feel no comparison needed, no requirement, to feel neither a want nor a need to respond to, only to be deliberate in this place to feel as it is to be called forth to present to you again this as an opportunity to peruse into. To be the determiner, the qualifier, the giver, the response needed. It is in this adequate way that we are to feel you the most.

Be disciplined here we say, for it is here in this voice, this voice of one that is to outperform many in if ever a comparison was to be made or suggested. It is a voice of hesitation yes that lingers uncertain, undecided whether to step forward once more or again. It is a place of deep desire, a relinquishing to the hardened self, the despised self, a hesitation to ignore the voice of old, the description of old, the comparisons of old, it is you here in this voice of distinguished distinction that one must be allowed to present to self to hear of it again.

❖ A fully qualified version of perfection.

❖ A voice that is no substitute ever for another.

❖ A fully comprehendible conversation that is held once more.

❖ A deliberate space of awareness.

An innate opportunity to peruse, acknowledge, satisfaction, contentment and determination belongs here in this you, in this voice of distinct opportunity.

The Art of Channelling.

IS simply this information that we are to disclose to you again, for it is a hidden aspect within you if not most that are to hold this as tried and true.

A version yes perhaps in as a disqualified or disillusioned starter of interpretation to have begun. To feel as to fumble and bumble ones way along blindly almost. To feel this as inaccessible by you. It is here we are to tighten up the reins shall we say, to allow for ones grip to soften and loosen along the way, to feel this forward movement of presence, a direction to be given, an allowance to be made, a descript to become. For it is in here this gift, this art, this allocation is yours to become to begin again into. This awareness of deliberate space, deliverance in awe of all it is that you are in this that you have become.

Allow for the opening to begin, the removal of the heaviness that has held you down or deep, constricted in as a human concept of thought to be yours to begin. An emotional attachment yes to this voice that is to proclaim outwardly of all it is that one is and is not. It is in the removal of this voice that is holder of 'the is not' that is hardest to let go of or not believe.

We are a placement within this one as a comprehension to understand a voice of steady, a magnificence to portray, a perfection in this performance to feel allocated an ability to align into once more. It is a comprehension yes in which many of you are to forego, to be undisciplined in, unseeing, even uninterested.

It is this that we are to portray to you outwardly in this way; for it is this that many of you are to feel of it as a performance of sorts, an opportunity to express an inner world that is a defiance within many of you to suggest it to be truth and harmony in all that is to exist. It is a space or a place to hold self in, to feel this limitless, boundless opportunity to receive once more.

To feel yes common placed in as an essence to describe of you to meld, and form into this formless suggestion once more, a place of proposition, a place of prosperity, an opportunity to begin again.

One must understand this in as a way of belief within oneself to trust again, to feel this format of self, this human embodiment as it is to release its hold on those reigns, to soften ones presence or grip upon this reality or version of self that has been lived.

A performance like no other yes; one of grand interpretation to explore and experience. A sensing from within that is to become again a requiring to revisit once more, a place of pleasant satisfaction, the ability to see out to view or observe of all that is comprehendible by you. A place of dedication to exist into, a sensing within this self to be reborn.

The Art of Channelling.

IS to re-enter, to become again this voice of grand interpretation.

To fulfill a prophecy of dedication that is yours to become knowing of again.

A knowing line of conversation or interpretation. An alignment, attunement, evolvement, empowerment. This is the *Art of channelling*, a recognition again into all it is that is. All it is that one must be forever and ever to see, to recall, to remember. To remind. A determination yes; as it is to begin to feel as it is to unravel, to reveal, to flow, to feel this as it is to impress this within you, a place of dedication to begin, to perform, to expect. Once allowed to open, to reveal the formatting of this old self is to simply disappear we shall offer to suggest in as an old sustainability that is to no longer serve of you as best. It is a hesitation yes, to feel as one is to hear and respond to this voice of love and reconnect, a recognition that is yours to become from a voice held deep within this comparativeness, comparing often of this to another, to feel to falter as in to listen to a conversation that does not serve you in the most adorable way. It is this sensing of this void that is to reveal to open to feel as it is to impact and inlay you in this way to feel like a chrysalis that is to create, to outperform, to shine the greatest, sparkling and reflecting as it attracts the energy and the light. Knowing that this is an opportunity to feel this reborning again, this reinstatement we shall offer, this place of pleasant pleasure to sit into, to dwell into to become once more, a voice of substance, a voice of sustainability, a voice of satisfaction, a voice of self service.

A voice where dreams are desires, where all opportunities lay, a place where one may call ones attention back to sit into instantly upon this *Art of channelling* to be remembered.

*To desire
is to dream...
&
to ask
is to receive...*

The Art of Channelling.

IS given to you like this; a discipline, a dedication that is to become formed within you again. A reliance to be spoken of as words of truth, words of value, words of dedication to you. It is a discipline within you yes as a form of disciple to appear in as this to encourage of self in this way, a prophecy, an entitlement, a description that is to surround and belong to all others in as an offering to have begun. It is the placement here in which it is that one has to be felt capturing of to call it forth, to call out to it, to become yours to know again. This integrated version, an uplevelling perhaps, to be considered by some to call of it to be. To feel as self is to manoeuvre, to make your way through this maze of life entrapment and catchment, to be considered your reality yes, a perception yes, a calling to yes, it is in this way that we describe the *Art of channelling* to be a deliverance like no other, a concept of self to be held in an abundance to feel in flow, an energy to wash over you.

To become this describer again in a voice that is viable and filled with opportunity, a compliance to self to know, to feel as a regulation from within to speak in this wonderous way. A place to touch, a place to hold perhaps to emphasis the heart here, in as a description to be called yours a willingness again.

The Art of Channelling.

IS a persuasion within most is it not?

To feel to hear this wanting, this voice of deliverance and deliberate.

It is to become yours once more upon ones stance or determination to feel this self in a righteous and worthy way. It is an encapsulation that has been present upon or within many of you in this reality of earth to present self and to perceive self as, a misguidance perhaps that has been delivered in a form of corruption or a convoluted self that is here to experience, to feel as this deformation is to take place, a respect like no other is to rally through you to become a description or a describing of you.

The Art of Channelling.

IS a voice. A gift given.

To hear and perceive of self in this way. This way of extraordinary, this way to see self in a humble yet indescribable way to feel of self-right and correct.

To feel steady and placed in this as an agreement within self to honour and obey. For it is this honouring and obeying that we are to suggest to you that has often been a misleading fact in as an honouring and obeying of those that are not of yours to depict as a consideration to follow. It is purely this peaceful act, this *Art of channelling*, this entwined flow, this intensity or thread of interwovenness that allows for you to feel this connection, this honouring, this openness, this awareness that is to become or make it self-known to you again.

This *Art of channelling* is you; it is you this spokesperson of all to be.

A forgiveness yes, a remembrance yes, a discipline yes, an opportunity yes, to be here in this fulfilment in as a becoming to witness, to observe, to serve and to interpret, to discover and explore once more. This valuable and viable impression of you in us to see.

We are a convoluted experience yes, to express as many waves of opportunity, to feel the folding and the unfolding as it is to become an immersion in this reality, an expression of self to speak a truth dedicated to you. A willingness and an awareness an opening, a gap shall we say that is allowed to open to feel as all is to enter to fill, to flow, to return. It is a place or concept within self to think as an extra or an adding to this that we are to describe as the *Art of channelling*, which is a self-impressed innate conversation, an ability within which you were designed.

An offering perhaps yes, in this as an opportunity to see yourself in this way, but a knowing deeply embedded, deeply enfolded within all it is that you are the simplicity of this that is.

The Art of Channelling.

IS received by all who are willing to listen, to sit, to feel this remembrance to stir within once more, as a place to sit, to stand, to feel steady in and believe upon again.

A place of deliverance and dedication to become yours knowing of once more. In truth it is to appear an exclusive few that are accommodating of this namely gift, this *Art of channelling*. It is this that we are to describe of an openness that is to appear within those that ask, it is to perceive of it as an art and act or gift by many that inhabit this reality. Know that it is this placement within that they are willing to place of themselves into again, this resonance, this higher essence, this higher self to be a description of love. An emphasis that is to flow yes, willingly into this as an apparatus of human to receive. A place to record, a place to remember, a place to enlighten again. To lift of self-up into this higher frequency or dimensions in as to capture this murmur, this sound, this dedication again. To feel as this vibration is to filter into ones perception.

To become known again, attuned to again. A voice like whisper, a murmur perhaps but yet a knowing of grand describe. A word that is a challenge in most to receive, to hear to speak, to be this love, this love guaranteed in the form of a conversation to describe as the *Art of channelling*.

We are a perception. A perception in this self to see, to be felt requested of or in this reality, this dimension to become yours to acknowledge again.

Sit in this presence, this recollection, this intuition that is yours to have never left or deserted you in as a way to describe of it in a human conversation to be had or held within, for of this we are to disagree it is not.

Let us offer a truth filled description of this presence for you.

Know of it as a placement within defined as excellence, perfectly timed, and designated within you to unravel, unfold, and reveal. A hidden treasure that is condensed in only as you to feel unworthy or unable to reveal its powerful reinstatement. A hinderance yes it is to appear upon this timely statement to be made as when and where. It is this that is a holding within most if not all that are to feel this as an indirect line or approach to experience.

The Art of Channelling.

IS when one can describe this self as simply to be.

To feel unhindered or distracted to see.

Limitless in this version of self to explore, to revisit all that IS.

In ones descript of self, one must see this timeless piece of interaction, an energy of great interface, deliberate to express all worlds and universes with contribution.

It is in here that you are found; The deliverer to offer this majestic information that upon ones hearing of it again will fill the trill and thrill of the resonance that it offers.

It is a truth yes to realise, for it is of many moments that have been wasted in this your time to have not believed in a voice as viable even possible to exist, let alone to call of it your own. This you must know, it is.

In truth it is this that we speak herein a depth of desire that is to be called your own, a vibration that is to filter and flow easily in and out of this energetic-ness that is to be considered home. It is a descript that we have likened to ourselves to feel as in a comfort and love to know of it as your own. One must become again dedicated to this viewing, this self to see in this astronomical way, yes a description that at times can feel too big of an ask to comprehend self as, it is this that you must.

See self here through this that we are the elevators of self into a realm far greater than you thought conceivable, a choice once more to revisit and feel this encouragement as it is to flow through you. A response such as this to be felt as joy, love, peace and happiness, an expression of this self that many in this time space reality are asking to receive. Believe in this that you are. Truth. Decidedness to reappear, confusions that lay deep but must be honoured in their timely release.

Hear self now. Feel self now. Allow self now.

You are this becoming once more.

Feel the delight in these words, they are yours to give self-credit to, for they are you in this becoming once more to revisit, to ask to see in this extraordinary way, a way of loved to feel free abandonment towards all that is to be yours to see.

The Art of Channelling.

IS when one believes in this as a token of opportunity, it then becomes this wise voice of reason and anticipation, which is to unravel and reveal to you finding its way forth. It is a description yes purely of anticipated connection again, and it is in this way that we are to state this *Art of Channelling* as to be the voice of giveance, the voice of god impress, a sustenance perhaps from within, that is to nurture you, to equip you with the knowledge of agreeance, acclamation, and receivership again.

To recognise this within oneself as to be the deliberate speaker, a seer of all in an observation to be had. To feel this infinite ability to connect again, to awe, to be in this as a a simplicity to exist here present in this very moment of your now.

We describe this as you; a presence, a simplicity to be, to feel, to find this voice of love enraptured & encompassed within this self to explore. A version of you yes perhaps hesitant to open the door, to tap upon the window, to even view inside, for it is often in this description of self that many of you are to hide, the innocent, the unheard, the debilitated, the version of you that is to crave a description of love to be heard. We speak to many of you in this way as a contraption {human- disciplined} with the ability still to hear this voice that is to erupt from inside, a reconnection point, a point of alliance to begin again, a vision of self in this place of high esteem, and awareness that is to become yours to belong into again.

A suggestion given perhaps to be of or from a better place, a realisation in this to exist in an outward more forward progressing way. It is a truth that is held within many of you here in this as a present-day moment to present, that are yet to feel as though they are to be uncovered, unearthed, to allow for it to feel as it is to make its way, as a burst of inspiration to the surface, asking to be explored. Feeling almost like a reinvention to begin, a reinvention in which one sees to describe of this self as magnificent. Once more in alignment with the greater self, the greater being, the god of all that is. This pure essence in which we hear the many of you proclaim eagerly that you are not and are to hold self away or apart from with a refusal to describe of self in this pure lighted way.

For it is a magnificent mastering is it not? To know that you are this extraordinary being of lighted emphasis and impress, an extravagance like no other, a dedication to become a suggestion from within the all to explore.

You are this radiant being, this god filled essence, this flow of inspirational love, this is the *Art of Channelling* to be spoken of as yours in a loving truth to receive.

Sit here now in this place or space to receive, align with a dedication to begin, a sensing from within self to explore, to feel a collaboration as it is to become yours once more. A yearning, an asking, or a desire to feel this presence, to feel this space as it is to light up within you. Hesitant at first yes to be seen, but deliberate to become, for it is in here in which it is that we are to suggest to you in many timelines, you are a forward progression that is becoming an awareness, an elaboration within you to consider, a collaboration within you in us in all, a choice or a choosing to be once more again this voice of recognition, this powerhouse of suggestibility to define of self in this gloriously lighted version, this impress of love.

For it is in this way that we describe this as the *Art of Channelling*.

The reasoning into and of all that is.

A voice of recollection again, a truth to be spoken, an alliance with the greatness, the greater being, the greater good, the great god of all that is. An impact within self like no other. An insurgence of self to discover once more. A place or a concept of self-yes in as a thought to be, to be this becoming, this choosing, this asking to receive, for it is in truth yes that we are to define you in this way, as a precise opportunity to sit, to receive, to listen, to ask, for it is in this awareness that it is to begin.

A space or a place to comprehend of self as more, this divine version of love, this giveance, divinity, an enlightenment, a celestial being, a connection to the most powerful place that is to exist 'creation.' Creation of the divine one in all to be the spokesperson in you again in this that we are to see ourselves as. A description yes like no other, a defining like no other, a description like no other to feel as this imprint is to rise from within you.

Speak these words of love, for it is in these words in which it is that you are to find your voice, this voice that acts as a gift for the *Art of Channelling*.

A description of you more powerful than one could ever imagine in this human form to speak of self as. A realisation again that you have stepped back into this timeline, this time space reality to view of self again in this wonder filled way, in as a wonderment to encourage, to experience and to grow and expand, to review and assess all that one is to become.

It is in truth yes; a way forward to describe of it as a journey, {human life impressed} that is to just begin for it is in a sensing within self to explore, to feel at times defeated and raw, to feel as though the battle has been lost. It is here that we are to remind you in this voice of love, that you are to feel this expectation as an anticipation to begin again. To feel the truth as it is to infuse you with a voice of great and powerful recognition into this as the *Art of Channelling* which flows forth out of you in as a voice of greater concept of all it is that you are.

The Art of Channelling.

IS this LOVE in you?

Acknowledge this self finally in this truth to be spoken of as yours.

Desire this descript to rise again, a letting go perhaps required of this great hesitation that hinders your exploration, but one that in certain will replenish you exuberantly upon its allowance to be received in a truth as yours.

Speak of self here now as the all that is to be IS.

Channelling is an innate form of communication delivered through, in and of the highest levels. You are all equipped with this knowledge, this explicit version of you is in truth the responder to ALL in this to know.

A powerful resonance that delivers to you once more your voice of wisdom & truth in grandeur love to be felt and known.

A truth spoken version of you.

Another reality perhaps?

One that is known by you, in this form of highest self to achieve.

You are knowing are you not of this voice? The eternal ever present & most powerful divine loved expression that becomes the determiner of ALL that IS.

In joyous blessings it is us in this that you BE.

Received & written with Gratitude May 2024.

MORE BOOKS BY AUTHOR TANYA TURTON.

Journey Of the Yellow Feather

Beautiful You Within Me

Angels Of Truth We Are

My Heart Speaks

Wanting To Be Me

Honouring Thy Self

My Way, the Truthful Way

Believing in ME

www.ingramcontent.com/pod-product-compliance
Lightning Source LLC
Chambersburg PA
CBHW062043290426
44109CB00026B/2720